T0017970

Gothic Guidance and **Macabre Musings** from
Your **Favorite Addams** Family Member

What
Would

Do?

IPHIGENIA JONES

ULYSSES
PRESS

Published by:
ULYSSES PRESS
PO Box 3440
Berkeley, CA 94703
www.ulyssespress.com

ISBN: 978-1-64604-654-6
Library of Congress Control Number: 2023943943

Printed in the United States
10 9 8 7 6 5 4 3 2 1

Acquisitions editor: Casie Vogel
Managing editor: Claire Chun
Project editor: Shelona Belfon
Editor: Renee Rutledge
Proofreader: Joyce Wu
Design and layout: Winnie Liu
Artwork: from Shutterstock.com—cover border © AntonGu; Wednesday and crows © Cattallina; vines with rose and folio © paprika; letter section icons © Daria Korolova

To Charlie, Addison, Bailey, and most especially, Savannah, whose spooky ideas have been woven through this book like a wonderful spiderweb. May you always be just who you are, just like Wednesday.

Contents

Introduction

As we make the treacherous journey through life and death, there will come many a time when we will need guidance. Seeking advice from trusted family members, empathetic friends, and wise mentors will ease our burdens and give us a beacon of light to help us down our path. Occasionally, we may not want the advice of someone with such noble intentions. Sometimes we seek not the light to illuminate the path ahead, but instead some instruction on how best to enjoy the shadows.

This is when to turn to the most severe little girl in the history of pop culture—Wednesday Addams. While perhaps not known for her moral fiber, Wednesday has bestowed advice to those around her in many documented instances. From teaching Lurch how to dance in the 1960s television show to providing investigative tips in the Netflix hit *Wednesday*, our ghastly girl has offered guidance for years.

Perpetually beloved outcasts, the Addams family as a whole has a strong sense of identity. They may not make choices deemed traditional by the outside world, but they are guided by their strong inner compasses (which are, of course, ruled by darkness). If you want advice that is perhaps outside the box, an Addams will give you encouragement that can help you navigate the world while remaining true to your inner self.

Not all advice will pertain to you directly, but will inspire you to begin thinking about the best ways to snap your existence into the life of your dreams (or nightmares). While Wednesday's actual advice may often be to devour your enemies, we have toned down some of the more murderous intent to better suit your day-to-day journeys. Of course, some treacherous tips might sneak through. We implore you to use your own discretion regarding revenge.

If all else fails, remember the Addams family credo: *Sic gorgiamus allos subjectatos nunc*, or "We gladly feast on those who would subdue us." Now, let's dig in.

Which Wednesday?

Several iterations of Wednesday Addams have manifested throughout the years. Wednesday first appeared as a grim little girl in *The Addams Family* comics by

Charles Addams. The comics ran in *The New Yorker* from 1932 until Addams's death in 1993, and featured an unusually gothic family that served as a satirized take on the ideal American family. The individual members of the family were unnamed until Charles Addams named them for the television show starting in 1964.

The original Wednesday of the comics was a macabre but seemingly content child who enjoyed making sure the fire was well lit on Christmas Eve in case Santa came down, viewed cemeteries as a family, and admired her deadly but witty mother, Morticia.

The comic's popularity led to the creation of the sitcom in the 1960s, which was intended to be more kooky and zany and less scary. This is where we get a lot of our classic Addams family details. The family's names and characters like Cousin Itt and Thing were created by Charles Addams for the show. One of the comic panels shows the iconic "Beware of the Thing" sign, and when asked by the show's producers what "the Thing" was, Addams suggested it be a disembodied head that traveled through the house on pulleys. That idea was discarded for a few reasons regarding "taste," and they compromised on a disembodied hand. (Another fun note: Thing was usually played by Ted Cassidy, who also played Lurch. He usually portrayed Thing as a right hand, but occasionally would use his left hand just to see if anyone would notice.) In general, the family was toned down to be silly rather than frightening, with the producers wanting a "less evil" approach to the characters. Wednesday was perhaps the happiest in this iteration, with a fairly cheerful nature even as her passions, such as raising spiders and guillotining dolls, remained deliciously macabre.

The 1991 and 1993 Barry Sonnenfeld films returned Wednesday to her more grim nature, as well as added her deadpan wit and overtly murderous intentions. This version, portrayed flawlessly by Christina Ricci, would become the standard for future adaptations, with Wednesday often being the standout favorite of the frightening family. Animated television adaptations followed, as well as a Broadway musical and 2019 CGI animated film. While the comics, original television show, and '90s films depict Wednesday as absolutely content in her place within the Addams home, many of the adaptations that followed explore Wednesday's desire to seek out a new place for herself.

Perhaps she did find a spot all to herself—in the 2022 Netflix adaptation, *Wednesday*. Here, the titular character is reimagined as a stoic aspiring author sent to a deliciously gothic school for outcasts. This version of Wednesday, as imagined by the talented Jenna Ortega, finds herself solving mysteries, befriending and battling monsters in turn, and finding a way to remain true to herself while finding her own path.

Why has Wednesday captured so many of our hearts? Besides her impeccable style and quick wit, she also provides a departure from tradition. For so many of our cultural touchstones, our little girl characters are inarguably Good. While they may be a little mischievous, our popular little girls live in what is Appropriate. As they grow, they learn lessons taught to them by the older and wiser that make them more palatable to the public. Many of their unusual quirks and hobbies are stamped out of them as they grow and change, often into an acceptable love interest. Wednesday is an enigmatic little girl, and remains so. She is allowed to be dark and strange, and we celebrate her for it. While many little girls have to learn to navigate the world of polite pastels, Wednesday remains dark and dreary. She remains unapologetically herself, and her family encourages her and loves her just as she is. For many little girls who saw themselves as witches, Wednesday never loses her magic.

This book seeks to combine many aspects of all these Wednesdays, as well as some input from her more macabre family members. While each adaptation has a unique take on the character, every Wednesday features a capable young woman with a lot of power within herself. We hope to lend some of her power to you.

Agony Aunts

This book features a collection of letters from people seeking advice, similar to an advice column in a newspaper or magazine. For hundreds of years, anonymous letter writers have sent in questions to a columnist, often colloquially called an "agony aunt." As the Addamses are all experts in agony, it seems only suitable to look to them for advice.

Because Wednesday Addams is so busy solving murders and committing crimes, we have taken it upon ourselves to thoroughly research every piece of Addams family media and apply our expertise to solving the problems presented by the letter writers. We present here letters from various perplexed citizens, and our responses as informed by the Addams family.

We intended to write responses as close to how we believe Wednesday and her family would respond; however, our lawyers have insisted on providing additional notes in order to keep our advice "legal" and "moral" and "not enticing of riots." We reluctantly agreed to these notes, though they may temper some of the efficacy of our gothic guidance.

Enjoy. If you have any questions you, yourself, would like to ask us, whisper your predicament into the nearest crystal ball and be sure to read your tea leaves for a response.

CHAPTER 1
FAMILY ADVICE

Introduction

The Addams family is about many things: gothic decor, quirky humor, frightening the neighbors. But above all, it is about a nuclear family with a deep love for one another, consisting of Gomez and Morticia, a very happily unhappy married couple, their two beloved children, Wednesday and Pugsley, and a live-in extended family that includes a grandmother (Eudora Addams and Griselda Frump are the two grandmothers, and which lives with the family depends on the iteration) and Uncle Fester, Lurch the butler, and a "handservant" named Thing. Historically, they may have appeared morbid and cold to the outside world, but their bond as a family has remained incredibly strong.

The family sees its challenges across every genre in which their story is told, from the Broadway musical and 2019 cartoon to the Netflix TV series. All show Wednesday attempting to strike out on her own, while the 1991 and 1993 film versions portray the family's devotion to Uncle Fester. The 1960s and 1990s television shows display various minor squabbles resolved in the 33-minute intervals, with the family always finding a way to return to each other. Wednesday may have her brief breaks with her family, but she always returns back home. She's the perfect person to seek out for family advice.

Surrounded by darkness, the Addams family finds comfort in a familial bond that makes up the core of who they are.

Dear Agony Aunt,

My cousin is floating in to spend some time in my family's crypt this summer. I can't stand her constant melodious singing or the bluebirds that arrive to braid her hair every morning. Moreover, her color palette is offensive to my eyes. How am I supposed to manage having her in the coffin next to me for two whole weeks?

Cordially yours,

Hardly Related

Dearest Hardly Related,

Familial obligations can often be painful, and unfortunately, terribly annoying. When we are lucky, family supports us through times of need and strife, joins us in laughter, and appreciates the assistance of our blade on a battlefield. When we are unlucky, family requires guest visits. However, you may be surprised to learn that not all differences are insurmountable. A mere glance at the Addams family tree shines a rather sparkly spotlight on Ophelia Frump, the blond-haired, floral-crowned elder sister of Morticia. Morticia and Ophelia are quite different, both in regard to style and personality; while our morbid Morticia is incisive and even-keeled, Ophelia is often flighty and occasionally downright cheerful. However, Morticia does her best to help Ophelia in finding love or a suitable career. The sisters may be different, but they share common ground in a desire for romance and ambition.

Another example of finding common ground within the Addams family is of the pastel-clad Debbie Jellinsky from the 1993 film *Addams Family Values*, in which she marries Uncle Fester for his money. Though her blond hair, perky attitude, and love of pastels promised friction, the Addamses were delighted to discover Debbie's penchant for murder and chaos. Unfortunately, it did not work out between Uncle Fester and Debbie, not because of Debbie's love of Barbie dolls, but instead due to her sloppy attempt to murder the entire family via a powerful surge of many electrical volts.

Finally, and perhaps most relevant to your situation, is the case of Enid Sinclair, Wednesday's roommate in the Netflix adaptation, *Wednesday*. Enid is cheerful, colorful, and loquacious—hardly a fitting friend for our young fiend. But throughout the course of the show, the roommates make an effort to find common ground. They share a competitive streak that helps them in the Poe Cup, and they work together to solve a mystery. It did require *effort*, my dear crypt keeper. Enid did not make Wednesday a rainbow-colored snood, but a black one in order to connect with Wednesday's sensibilities. When Enid first began helping Wednesday with her investigation, Wednesday ordered Thing to keep the smelling salts handy in case Enid had a fainting spell. Each knew how to bring the other into their world while keeping a thought for the other's needs.

So perhaps, my dear, you could make a bit of an effort with your effervescent relation. Inquire of her bluebirds— do they perhaps know the birds who plucked out the eyes of Cinderella's stepsisters in the original gruesome tale? Perhaps they could introduce you to the local corvids of the neighborhood, as a raven familiar could be useful some mornings to do your own braids. If your cousin is a baker (as many singing maidens are), perhaps she could show you the best baked goods in which to hide a poison. Shared blood alone does not make finding common ground easy, but even a small effort will go a long way.

If you make an honest effort to connect with your cousin and still find no joy in her company, consider these two weeks a practice run in withstanding torture—a useful skill in all young people's lives. Fill your time plotting your eventual revenge for when you are both adults. A dish best served cold takes years to prepare, after all.

Detestably yours,
A Blood Relative

Dear Wicked Weekday,

I really want a pet. My parents say I'm not ready, but I think I am! How can I convince them that I deserve a pet?

Thank you!

Animal Admirer

Darling Animal Admirer,

You've chosen an enlightened path, that of the lover of beasts. The Addams family has a long history of being wonderful pet owners of a myriad of creatures. Let's take a look, shall we?

Pugsley claims ownership of one of their most beloved pets, Aristotle the octopus. Aristotle has been featured in the comics and the 1960s television show. He is very friendly and affectionate, and the affection is returned; Gomez bathes him in the tub, and Morticia is often seen knitting many-legged little sweaters for him. Other aquatic pets that exist around the family are Wednesday's octopus Socrates in the 2019 animated film, and a giant squid named Bernice in the Broadway musical.

Another beloved pet that appears in many adaptations is the treasured lion named Kitty Kat. Kitty Kat often appears wandering through the family house, frightening visitors and amusing the family. Morticia is often seen treating her carnivorous plants, such as her favorite plant, Cleopatra, in ways similar to pets. The family also has various vultures and a pair of piranhas.

Wednesday herself has multiple pets of her own. She is particularly fond of spiders, including one named Homer. In the *Wednesday* show, she fondly remembers her cherished scorpion, Nero, who was tragically killed by a bicycle.

Now, in your parents' defense, taking care of pets is very difficult. Remember to look after them regularly, lest they get rings under their tentacles as Aristotle does when sleep deprived. You may have to put aside your own interests in this regard—Pugsley ignores Aristotle when he joins Scouts, and Wednesday loses playtime privilege with Homer as punishment when she uses Uncle Fester's dynamite. You must remember to walk them regularly, as Wednesday would do with Nero while he was still with her. Feeding your pet is also necessary, of course–Morticia provides Cleopatra with a steady diet of zebra burgers and yak meatballs.

Here is our recommendation for convincing your parents: Work on proving your capacity for responsibilities. Take up more of the household chores. Try collecting the belladonna from the poison garden without being asked. Keep your room clean. Offer to cook dinner in the cauldron, and be sure to clear your plate after playing with your food. Do not draw attention to this—do *not* say something in the realm of, "Look at how I am sweeping up the snakeskins! Don't I deserve a pet?" Subtly manipulating your parents requires discretion.

After a few months of this, visit the discussion of a pet again. Bring your research. Dig deep into the archives of your dustiest library and find the pet that best suits your current lifestyle. If you live a quiet lifestyle of spell-casting and studying, perhaps a traditional cat familiar would work best for you. Research various breeds and find one that thrives in your current environment; for example, do not ask for a night-blooming carnivorous plant if you live in one of those towns cursed with constant daylight.

Present to your parents your ideas. We recommend giving this presentation in a haunted theater and asking the ghosts to whisper encouragements to your parents. Remain calm and poised. Remember how steady Wednesday is, and emulate her. Listen to your parents' concerns, which may be valid and bring up points you did not consider. Perhaps they've experienced owning a jackalope and know that they are very difficult to catch and also hide under couches all day. If your parents still say no, I apologize. Remember this, and when you grow up, create an entire menagerie.

Good luck.

With love,
Wicked Weekday

Sinister Sister,

My aunt disapproves of my "lifestyle." She calls me all the time to tell me why I'm living my life wrong because of the person I love. She complains to my parents about how my life is immoral. We're going to be together for family dinner on the upcoming holiday. My girlfriend cannot come, so it'll just be me. What can I do?

Sadly,
Neglected Niece

Neglected Niece,

Block her number. Tell your parents that you do not want to hear about her complaints, and ask them to limit the information they provide her about you and your partner. Ask your family to change the subject with her if she brings you up. Do not attend family functions if she is also invited.

If you must attend a family function with her for whatever reason, steal a glass that she has been holding (use gloves). Break the glass and put it in your food. When surrounded by witnesses, "find" the glass and gasp. Bring out your personal fingerprint kit and match her finger-prints to the glass in your food. Accuse her in front of everyone. If you can faint, do so. She will be shamed and possibly placed in the stocks.

Come to our solstice instead. Bring your girlfriend and we will all dance under the moon.

Love,
Sinister Sister

NOTE: Our lawyers think this is an "overreaction" and "logistically impossible" and "definitely illegal" and "stocks don't exist anymore." We have been encouraged to instead suggest "ignoring your aunt" and "walking away" when she attempts to interact with you. Something about a high road and establishing boundaries. We think framing her for attempted murder would naturally create a boundary (as she'd be locked in stocks), but our lawyers insist that ignoring her at family functions is a "healthier and more legal" action.

If you do ignore her at these functions, we also recommend telling trusted family members of your intentions. Ask them to help you by engaging her in distractions, pulling you into long conversations that cannot possibly be interrupted, or asking you to run out and get more ice. Every function always needs more ice. Good luck. The invitation to our solstice remains open.

Dear Abbey,

My twelve-year-old granddaughter is in desperate need of a hobby. She is a very bright girl, and I would like to encourage her into proper activities. I am looking for hobbies that only the most accomplished and appropriate young ladies participate in.

Thank you,
Concerned Grandmother

Dear Concerned Grandmother,

We believe you have intended to write to another advice column. Due to the misspelling of the advice columnist's name, the postman assumed you were referring to the haunted abbey next door to our crypt and the letter found its way to us. As we do not print our replies in traditional newspapers, we hope our method of response does not alarm you. The blood on your walls will drip down nicely to form a beautiful occult symbol after you have read this to completion. Don't worry, we will ensure that it is a proper occult symbol that is sure to endure all manners of cleaning methods.

To address your concerns in your letter—we completely empathize. Imagine Morticia and Gomez's horror when they discovered Pugsley had joined the Scouts, or the time the children attempted to make fudge. We will help prevent your granddaughter from doing things like joining clubs or baking. Let's look into some more appropriate hobbies for young ladies—and for others. While the 1960s television show revolved around some strict gender norms, let's agree that "girl interests" or "boy interests" do not exist. There is only darkness. Here are some Addams-approved hobbies:

† Model trains
† Blast fishing
† Electrocutions
† Guillotine building and practice
† Potions (This would be a useful hobby to encourage if your granddaughter has demonstrated an interest in baking.)
† Demolitions
† Necromancy (Speaking to the beyond would be an excellent notation on a college application, as we hear that many universities are interested in communications.)
† Robotics
† Art (Morticia was a sculptor, and the Addams home is filled with portraits. Also, imagine the glorious mess your granddaughter could make.)

- † Torture
- † Knitting (Morticia is often seen making many-legged sweaters for her future offspring and the family's pet octopus.)
- † Cryptozoology
- † Collecting (Pugsley steals road signs; Wednesday collects spiders.)
- † Weaponry (Sword fights and fencing are an Addams family tradition. Morticia and Gomez adore dueling one another. Affectionately, of course.)
- † Botany (particularly carnivorous or poisonous plants)
- † Dance (Many members of the Addams family dance, as detailed in a letter later on.)
- † Linguistics (Members of the family can speak a wide variety of languages, including Spanish, French, Italian, German, Latin, and Cousin Itt.)
- † Martial arts

Importantly, Morticia and Gomez make efforts to support their children, even when they disagree with their interests. For instance, in the *Addams Family Values*, when their baby, Pubert, demonstrates interest in things such as Dr. Seuss, Morticia manages to bring herself to read *The Cat in the Hat* to him. Even if your grandchild is interested in something horrible like...team sports, remember that your support is the most important thing you can offer. Pushing too hard will lead to rebellion, and then you may end up having to attend a sweet sixteen party with the theme of cheerleading.

Be kind. Fake an interest if you must. Remember there are no such things as "proper" children with "proper interests." There is always only a child who wants your support. And possibly your blood for summoning spells.

With love,

Not Abbey

Dear Detestable Dramatist,

My brother has begun dating someone new. She seems very nice from his stories, but she doesn't speak the same language as I do. We can't understand each other, but I want her to feel welcome when she comes over next week! It'll be my first time meeting her. How can I help?

From,

Morosely Monolingual

Dear Morosely Monolingual,

While we cannot relate—Wednesday and the family speak many languages—we do appreciate your intent to welcome a new person into your home and family. Learning new languages is good for your brain and for society, so it would be beneficial to attempt to learn some of her language. It is so nice to possess another form of communication. Think of how many more enemies you will be able to threaten with an additional language.

However, we assume you are merely human and unable to learn another language with fluency within a week. We recommend picking one or two phrases to look up and practice, such as "Hello," "Nice to meet you," "I like your blood-stained gown," etc. The internet is a treasure trove of information and will likely offer videos on how to pronounce your chosen phrase. We assume your brother knows some of her language, so ask him for tips. It is always humiliating to ask a sibling for help, but consider this a necessary evil. (We like only unnecessary evils.)

Many family members on the Addamses family tree are multilingual. Of course, the Addamses have a special gift of understanding many unusual languages. While we as the audience are not invited to understand, the Addamses have no problem conversing with family members like Thing or Cousin Itt.

Cousin Itt is, interestingly, a family member not originally created by Charles Addams, but a brand-new character created for the original sitcom. He is covered in long hair, with a hat and sunglasses to add some pizzazz. He speaks an unusual language with a high tone and rapid speed. While the Addamses have always understood him, people outside the family cannot parse what he is saying. In an episode of the original sitcom, Cousin Itt learns to speak with a low baritone voice and is comprehensible to others. As outsiders begin to fawn over his new deep voice, his personality changes and he becomes rude and overly critical. The family is thrilled when, at the end of the episode, his voice returns to normal. They are happy to meet Cousin Itt where he's at, and love him just as is, with his own language and all.

Thing does not use a voice to communicate. He seems to communicate through a combination of his own sign language, knocks and snaps, Morse code, and written language. Whatever he is trying to say, the Addamses make an effort to understand him (and are usually successful fairly immediately). Thing is, of course, a beloved member of the family, and his unique ways to communicate are as a part of him as his five fingers.

All this is to say, languages are wonderful. They teach us about other people, other cultures, and ourselves. It might seem awkward at first learning to communicate when you do not share a language in common, but there are so many ways to be welcoming. Wednesday does not welcome anyone with a smile, but her parents certainly do. If you're more like Wednesday and are not a smiler but still want to extend a welcome to your brother's partner, your best (but stoic) interpretation of a phrase from her language will help. Ask your brother about her interests. Is there a particular dessert that she likes or a favorite instrument of torture? You can do this. You (presumably) love your brother and want to embrace his partner, and those two things will go a long way.

Con cariño,
Detestable Dramatist

Dear Nightmare Novelist,

My sibling is about to have a child! I want to be a good uncle, but I don't have any aunts and uncles of my own to know how to do that. How can I be a good uncle to the newest hellion in my family?

With relative affection,
Unusual Uncle

Dear Unusual Uncle,

Terribly unhappy news. Please give your sibling our wishes for a very spooky child. Lucky for you, you have come to one of the most...radioactive uncles in popular culture. Uncle Fester is most commonly known as Gomez's brother in stories across the Addams family oeuvre, and is, therefore, Wednesday and Pugsley's uncle. He often rots merrily in the background behind some of the more known family members, but the family would not be the Addamses without him.

Fester is a very odorous uncle and brother. In the original comics, he's rarely seen among the other family members. Notably, one of these rare instances is a panel in which he accompanies Wednesday and Pugsley on a blast fishing trip. Right away, we can tell you that spending time with your young relatives is the most valuable gift you can give them, whether that means catching fish with dynamite or taking them to a movie.

Fester is electric. We mean this quite literally, as he can conduct electricity. He most often demonstrates this by placing a lightbulb into his mouth to illuminate it and, thus, delight the children. Do you have any fun traits, Uncle to Be? Perhaps you can tell knock-knock jokes or juggle chainsaws. You have plenty of time to learn, as in our experience, children do not enjoy chainsaws until at least a few months old.

In the 1991 film, Fester suffers from amnesia and attempts to incorporate himself back into the family. He bonds with his niece and nephew over common interests: acting out Shakespeare's bloodiest death scenes, reading medical textbooks, and playing pranks with bones. He makes an effort to be there for the children, ensuring his attendance at their school play and providing them with plenty of prop blood to spray onto the audience. Once again, prioritize being there for the child. If you live far away from this part of your family, send letters and FaceTime. Ask about their hobbies and interests, and listen.

In the animated movies, we see some of Uncle Fester's bond with Pugsley. He assists Pugsley with his Caber Mazurka, a traditional performance for the family.

In the sequel, Fester provides Pugsley with plenty of romantic advice, including his book *The Fester Method: How to Woo and Other Tips on Love*. His advice is perhaps...misguided, but his efforts in helping his nephew are not unappreciated. Providing assistance when needed will make you beloved in the eyes of a child, especially if it is something you are an expert in, such as burying a body. Once again, you have time to hone your skills. A child will not require you to bury a body for them for at least 18 months.

In Netflix's *Wednesday*, Fester visits his titular niece while she attends school at Nevermore, and he is on the run. His affection for Wednesday is obvious. He wants to spend time with his pigtailed protégé, playing hide and seek in Enid's stuffed animals and helping with her investigation. He even refrains from eating bees for her, a true sign of his devotion. Before he departs, he tells her that she is his favorite. We see rare smiles from this version of Wednesday, and most of them are directed at Fester.

We can only encourage you to do as Fester does. Get lost in the Bermuda Triangle, put your head in a screw press to relieve headaches, and marry a serial killer determined to access your family's fortune. On second thought, those have little to do with his abilities as an uncle. Those are just for your own personal fun. To be a good uncle, do as Fester does: be there when they need you, show an interest in their lives, and listen.

With filial piety,
Nightmare Novelist

CHAPTER 2
RELATIONSHIP ADVICE

Introduction

Wednesday Addams is many things. She's calculating and cold, with a sharp wit and sharper knives. One thing she is not is particularly adept at relationships. She is close with her family, including with Lurch and Thing. She demonstrates her own violent form of affection for her brother Pugsley, and a deep admiration for both of her parents. Aside from that, we see glimpses of Wednesday developing tentative bonds with others.

Wednesday is a careful girl when it comes to matters of her closely guarded heart.

She cautiously makes friends, most notably Enid Sinclair in the Netflix adaptations. Wednesday and Enid slowly overcome their differences to build a strong bond, even exchanging an embrace.

When it comes to love, Wednesday has the most morbid model of marriage—the romance between her parents. Morticia and Gomez truly love each other. They understand each other on a fundamental level, encouraging one another and delighting in each moment they spend together. Wednesday, herself, finds various love interests across mediums, and we see a slightly different reaction from her in each iteration—from devotion to pity. We are eager to share her wisdom on friendship and romance.

Dear Double Braids,

My husband continuously grinds his fangs throughout the night, keeping me awake. When I shared this concern, he told me, "That sounds like your problem," and suggested I sleep on the couch. What can I do?

From,
Still Awake

Dear Still Awake,

Buy pliers.

From,
Double Braids

NOTE: Our lawyers have suggested that perhaps "pliers" was a misspelling of the words "mouth guard."

Dear Ghastly Girl,

I love to throw elaborate banquets for my coven and related friends. One witch in particular will always RSVP that she will attend, and then *never* shows. I don't have a large banquet hall and my coven members are many, so I must leave some people out. I like her a lot, but when she says she's going to come and then doesn't, it leaves an empty broom and hurts my feelings a little. Should I stop inviting her? What if she gets hurt that she's no longer receiving my invitations?

May the moonlight reveal all truths,
Party Planner

Dear Party Planner,

There are a few ways to handle this problem like a true Addams. The first is to cast a curse upon her, turning this erstwhile witch into a lovely wall sconce, so she will always be there to light up your parties. Wednesday would likely follow this course of action—she doesn't particularly enjoy large gatherings of people having fun. She'd prefer a light fixture in order to better read her death scrolls. But perhaps your banquet hall does not require any new decor and you'd like to continue to throw these...parties. We will assume you insist on throwing these affairs as a way to spy on your fellow witches and will proceed with our advice.

Perhaps stop inviting this witch to *every* banquet. Try inviting some of the other members you have not invited before. Your space is limited, but witches are not. If your absent witch inquires as to why she was not invited, be gentle but honest. Your space was limited and you wanted to invite someone else, but she is definitely on the guest list next time. If she continues to mislead you when invited, maybe continue to leave her off the list.

In the meantime, try inviting this witch to more intimate gatherings. Don't worry about filling your banquet hall to the brim. Invite one or two friends for a low-key stroll in the local graveyard. Perhaps she is shy around large groups and is reluctant to attend, or has difficulty finding goblin care for a long event. This will help relieve some of the party-planning stress on your shoulders—no extra food or brooms to worry about if she does not arrive.

You can also let your coven know your needs. On your next invitations, feel free to add a postscript indicating how many days in advance you need an RSVP, and that you'd appreciate accurate responses. Writing this in blood can really help get the message across.

Dear Full of Woe,

How can I tell if a girl likes me?

From,
Lovesick

Dear Lovesick,

She doesn't.

Sincerely,
Full of Woe

Dear Lovesick,

We have been informed that the above response may lead to heartbreak. Though we do not see why that is such a problem, as it is in all likely the truth of the matter, we will attempt to give more general advice for all the lovers.

Unlike her ultra-romantic parents, Wednesday has never been particularly amorous. She has had the occasional love interest, with reactions to them as different as the respective adaptations. She pities, protects, and kisses a bespeckled boy named Joel Glicker, who is allergic to everything. In the 2010 Broadway musical, Wednesday is engaged to a fairly normal college student named Lucas. This Wednesday allows Lucas to introduce her to new things, such as wearing colors and singing about her feelings. We can't relate, but she is allegedly happy.

In the first season of the *Wednesday* series, Wednesday is saddled with not one but *two* love interests: the mysterious and talented barista, Tyler, and the psychic artist, Xavier. With both of these supposedly dreamy teen boys, Wednesday works to solve mysteries in their unique small town. Will Wednesday be greeted with more love interests in future seasons of the show? Only time will tell.

The Wednesday of all of these love interests is unique to the adaptation. A commonality across all of them is the way Wednesday shows her interest. She lets herself be seen, displaying some sort of vulnerability. She shares her pastimes, such as including a love interest in her secret plan to turn a Thanksgiving play into a scathing indictment of colonialism. She makes time for the likes of a frightening viewing of a romantic comedy. Of course, Wednesday also spends time with people in order to keep track of suspects, so one must be wary.

To tell if a girl likes you, pay attention. Does she demonstrate foolish moments of vulnerability? Does she naively introduce you to her interests or spend time learning about yours? She may indeed like you, as a friend or as something more. The only way to know for sure is to ask, and to respect the answer given. Invite her on a date, be clear with your intentions, and either proceed with a potential new love interest or be content with having a friend.

With the fluttering of a bat's wings,

Full of Woe

To the Horrible Helper,

I have moved to a new town, and I'd like to make some new friends. I'm sure you'll tell me to join a hobby or club, but I only enjoy swimming in quicksand and there isn't a quicksand league in my new town.

Yours,

Alone in Quicksand

Dear Alone in Quicksand,

Making new friends is very simple. If you have the means to gather the necessary body parts and assemble them in time for your next lightning storm, we highly recommend making your own, brand new friend. We suggest exploring your new town's graveyards and sourcing local materials. In some Addams family properties, it's suggested that the family's butler, Lurch, was created in such a manner.

However, it can be a tedious wait for the perfect lightning storm. Let's take a look and see how Wednesday has made new friends in various episodes of *The Addams Family* and beyond. In the original television show, there are many episodes in which the family generously welcomes a neighbor into their wonderful home to delight in train crashes or their pet lion, Kitty Kat, only to have the prospective new friend run screaming out the door. Even when the Addamses attempt to help their neighbors by giving their drab home a beautifully gothic makeover, the neighbors are appalled.

There is something to be learned from this: not everyone has good taste. Instead of wasting your time on people who have no appreciation for aesthetics, focus your efforts on finding quality friends. Do not try to force the unrefined and uncultured to be your friends. Of course, this advice is not always easy to follow. It's been nearly sixty years and Morticia and Gomez have yet to learn this particular lesson.

This is not to say you should find only friends who share your limited interests. In Netflix's *Wednesday*, for example, Wednesday finds one of her most valuable allies when she joins the beekeeping club. Though Wednesday initially has little interest in the Nevermore Hummers, she takes a chance and finds a loyal and trustworthy friend in Eugene Ottinger, a passionate psychic. Trying a new hobby isn't always the worst idea. Sometimes it can even be quite painful, which we love.

You could also start your own quicksand club, which is sure to attract the beautifully bizarre type of people you want to meet. And if you don't like them, simply don't help them out of the quicksand to avoid any awkward conversation.

Always your friend,
Horrible Helping Hummer

NOTE: Our lawyers informed us that one has an obligation to help everyone in quicksand, even if you don't like them. We were just as startled to learn this as you! With this new information, we revised our last piece of advice: help them if they are trapped in quicksand, but be sure to find an exit strategy from any ensuing awkward conversation.

Dear Cunning Confidant,

I recently signed up for some dating apps in order to find true love. So far it's been a miserable landscape of confusion. Which apps are the best for finding hot singles?

Looking for Love

To Looking for Love,

Your moniker distresses us. We do not like most of your letter, except for the bit about a miserable landscape. How can we get to this vicious vista?

The Addamses have never met their partners on an app. We would also be interested in learning about whatever sort of an application could bring such spooky soulmates together, but we have not heard of one. We communicate using ravens or subliminal messages in television advertisements as opposed to smart phones.

Anyway, let's look at how the Addamses have met their individual paramours. As mentioned in previous responses, Wednesday has met young lovers in various locations: Nevermore Academy and the surrounding town of Jericho in the Netflix adaptation; while wandering in Central Park with a crossbow in the Broadway adaptation;

and as fellow misfits at Camp Chippewa in the 1993 film. Her responses to these young men all change depending on the context and characterization of our wicked wretch.

Pugsley rarely has love interests. However, in *Addams Family Reunion*, he meets a girl named Gina at the wrong family reunion, while in the animated film *The Addams Family 2*, he meets Ophelia, the pig-human hybrid daughter of a man mistakenly believed to be Wednesday's biological father. Pugsley seems most successfully to meet love interests at other people's family functions. Perhaps Pugsley's lesson in romance is to be willing to seek love in unusual locations.

Uncle Fester fares differently in love, as his various escapades often end in violence. He engages in several love interests throughout his varying portrayals, but luckily they usually end in heartbreak or murder. Most notably, Fester meets his wife, Debbie Jellinsky, when the femme fatale poses as a nanny for the Addamses. She marries him strictly for his money and attempts to murder him and his family. She is naturally our favorite of all his girlfriends, a perfect ballerina Barbie. Such a shame she wore so many pastels. Fester also has a pen-pal love interest in the original '60s television show, in which he attempts to lose weight in order to impress her for their first in-person meeting. Once she arrives, she is no longer interested in him, because he is too skinny. Let this be a lesson for you, longing lover: do not change yourself for the possibility of impressing someone. They are looking for your true if terrible traits.

Of course, the handsome Lurch and the dapper Thing have love interests. In the original sitcom, Lurch meets a friend of Morticia's and develops feelings for her, but things go awry when Grandmama has a mix-up with a love potion. In the 2019 animated series, Grandmama herself has a crush on Lurch.

Thing has one of the most consistent relationships across the series, which is with his love, Lady Fingers. Lady Fingers is a handmaiden and meets Thing when she accompanies her lady on a visit to the Addamses. In both Lurch's and Thing's cases, the idea is to have a friend set you up with another one of their friends. Similarly, Cousin Itt dates Morticia's sister, Ophelia, in the sitcom. In the '90s, he marries Margaret Alford after meeting her at the Addamses' home.

Finally, we come to Morticia and Gomez. An aspirational love story to goth couples everywhere, this dreadful duo has a few different origin stories. In the original sitcom, Gomez is expected to marry Morticia's sister, Ophelia, in an arranged marriage. Once Gomez and Morticia meet, however, it's clear to everyone that they are a much better match. (Don't feel too bad for Ophelia. She is happy to end their arranged engagement and attempts to pursue Itt.)

In the '90s film, Gomez dreamily recalls his and Morticia's first meeting at a funeral, in which Morticia was even more beautiful to him than the corpse. And we have yet another meeting in the Netflix adaptation—at Nevermore Academy. What can their first encounters tell us about finding a mate? Keep your eyes and hearts open; perhaps your paramour is waiting for you where you least expect it!

Does any couple love each other as much as Morticia and Gomez? Black hearts that understand each other, beating to the beat of the same funeral dirge? We wish you luck in finding such an enduring romance.

Reluctantly,
Gunning Confidant

Cunning Confidant Again,

I reached out to you about the dating apps and you gave me unrelated advice and a history lesson. I've given up on dating apps. You seem pretty pointless, but aren't you a witch or something? Can you tell me how to make a love potion?

From,
Looking for Love

To Desperate for Love,
Our love potions are incredibly successful and potent, but will we tell you how to make one? No. We would never inflict you on an unassuming public. Forcing someone to love you in particular is a form of torture even Wednesday would balk at.

 We recant our earlier statement wishing you luck.

Gunning Confidant

Eerie Evildoer,

I've been happily seeing my partner for a few months now, and I'd like to take them on a special date. What can I do to make a memorable night?

Love,

Pondering Paramour

Dear Pondering Paramour,

So many ideas. First of all, you should begin by taking them on a stroll through a graveyard. Do you know of any particularly glamorous crypts? Avoid those. Look for the crumbling ones, as they are far more romantic. They will remind your partner of how even a memorial to death is not eternal. The only thing that is eternal is your love and the all-encompassing darkness encroaching over the universe.

Wednesday herself has been on few dates, as she's usually quite young in media portrayals. She does take Joel Glicker on a walk through her family's crypt (only to attempt to scare him to death). In the Netflix adaptation, she is treated to a lovely date with Tyler in a crypt, where he makes her a nighttime picnic and watches a horror movie with her (*Legally Blonde*, possibly the most frightening movie Wednesday could imagine). Take notes from Tyler. Though he did end up betraying Wednesday, he did have good date ideas. A romantic picnic under the moonlight is a great idea.

Continuing with your walk through the crypt, arrive at your romantic picnic spot. Impress your partner with the spookiest food you can think of, either self-made or bought from a local apothecary. Watching a movie would also be a good addition, though perhaps you don't want to go as fearsome as Reese Witherspoon.

After your nighttime picnic, take a note from Gomez and Fester Addams. In *Addams Family Values*, the brothers take their dates to a local bistro. Order some creepy cocktails and enjoy the band (trapped behind bars, whether for their safety or the safety of the patrons remains to be seen). As the band strikes up a romantic tango, invite your partner to a dance, assuming you can dance. If you cannot, look deep into your partner's eyes and recite poetry in the most amorous language you can conjure.

After your walk, picnic, and bistro, it will likely be time to retire. Walk your partner to their home or mode of transportation and let them know it was the most sublime night of your life. Send a bat to ensure they've safely arrived home, and perhaps ask the bat to deliver a letter expressing to your partner your enjoyment of the great night.

If you frequently do these things, try doing something new. Try taking a class together, such as a painting, ceramics, or embalming class. Learn to cook a new meal together. Visit a local museum and plan a heist. These are just some common ideas for a lovely couple.

With love and darkness,

Eerie Evildoer

To My Misanthropic Muse,

I have a pretty girlfriend, but she's been very stressed lately and kind of a drag. Now there's another girl, who is always fun. I think I can date both of them without them knowing, but I'm not sure which I should invite to my upcoming birthday party. Do you have any ideas?

Sincerely,
Ready to *Romeo*

Dear Romeo,

Do you know what happened to Romeo? He died, dear reader. He drank poison. What do you think it tasted like, my ridiculous rake? Do you think it tasted a little bitter, perhaps like the coffee you're sipping on now? Did you notice that the barista who served you that coffee had long braids with a white collar peeking from under that green apron? How does that drink taste?

Anyway, while you consider this, we will be visiting your girlfriend. Perhaps she can meet your fun-loving young woman to help her relax and mourn the untimely end of her previous perilous relationship.

Enjoy your sips,
Nobody's Muse

NOTE: Our lawyers are apoplectic over this letter, for some reason. Let us be clear: Do not poison any possibly philandering boyfriends. There are many other people to date who are not awful and likely are much better at tasting possible arsenic. Our lawyers did not like this statement either. Do not poison anyone. We are merely telling a very funny joke. We love amusements and jests, don't you?

Chapter 3
Career

Introduction

One of the most stress-inducing aspects of our capitalistic society is our career life. So many aspects of work can be absolute agony. And while we approve of agony in general, we understand the way industry can drain one's energies, leaving little for your true passion of conjuring the undead.

The Addamses have an interesting relationship to employment. Gomez appears to have multiple streams of income as a business owner or possibly as someone with controlling interest in large banks. A major plot point of the 1991 film is a hidden vault containing the family's riches, indicating no need for day-to-day work. As you'll read in the following letters, Morticia, Lurch, and other members of the family have attempted various careers of their own as well. Their short-lived occupational adventures may not have yielded long-term careers but will provide you with plenty of guidance. Additionally, the Addams family also serve as employers to Lurch, their beloved butler, and Thing, their loyal handservant. Both Lurch and Thing have been with the family for an eternity, so one must assume the Addamses are equitable and fair employers.

As for our woeful protagonist, Wednesday spends her time aspiring to be a novelist. She works on it diligently, at least an hour per day. She also does well as a paranormal investigator, solving the supernatural murders of the small town of Nevermore. What career awaits Wednesday in the future? Only time (and tarot cards) may tell.

Dear Creepy Correspondent,

I'm about to graduate from my academy and I'm struggling to find a career that works for me. My parents want me to try the family business (possession) and/or a similar career (repossession), but I'm not sure what I want to do. Do you have any ideas to help me find my passion?

From,
Confused Career Hunter

Dear Confused,

Learning to navigate the working world is one of the most horrific aspects of adult life. The Addamses are often depicted as terribly wealthy and have tried their hands at many different careers. They are truly examples of successful jacks-of-all-trades, tackling a proliferation of professions. Gomez has worked in many fields to accumulate their massive wealth, and we see rare glimpses of his work life.

While very rarely shown actually working, Gomez owns many businesses all around the world, from crocodile farms to tombstone factories. He is also an attorney (voted Least Likely to Pass the Bar), and is involved with several banks. Interestingly, in 2008, *The Guinness Book of World*

Records named Gomez as the fifth-richest television character, with a net worth of $8.2 billion.

Morticia has also tried a perfectly manicured hand at various vocations. In the 1991 film, it's revealed that she studied spells and hexes (which her job interviewer clarifies as "liberal arts"). Across all the portrayals of the family, she has worked as a teacher of preschool as well as tango and fencing, a decorator, an author, and a sculptress. In the 1960s television show, she often reverts back to being a homemaker in order to spend time with the children. In one episode, she is horrified to realize they have turned to making fudge in her absence. We think that perhaps Gomez could have spent less time with his toy trains and more time helping so that Morticia could have enjoyed more time dedicated to a profession.

Both Morticia's and Gomez's mothers are practicing witches, as well as Morticia. Cousin Itt and Morticia's sister, Ophelia, both required help finding careers, trying roles such as marriage counselors, artists, and tour guides. The Addamses' butler, Lurch, has also been a pop star in his time.

All this is to say, Wednesday's single-minded determination to become a writer is unusual for not only an Addams, but many different types of creatures across the world. There is no need to rush into a single career, and there is no law saying you cannot change careers if you would like to. (Even if there were such a law, we'd delight in instructing you to break it.)

Life is for exploring all the possible horrors of the world. Why limit yourself to one catastrophic career when you could collect plenty of putrid pursuits? You are filled with the disgusting bloom of youth. Enjoy your slow parade toward death by trying different things. Try taking part in your family's business if you'd like, while perhaps attending mortuary school. Take a spin as a barista while also apprenticing with a psychic. Of course, we cannot all indulge in the march of capitalism like the super-wealthy Addamses do, so if you need to take a job you don't particularly like in order to survive, that is an ugly necessity. Explore passions in your free time—raising the undead is a free hobby.

With love and cash,
Creepy Correspondent

To Austere Advisor,

I love my job as a gardener, but I've recently become
a creature of the night. I'd prefer to start working the
graveyard shift, but I'm not sure how to approach my boss
about a change. Any suggestions?

> With apprehension,
> **Dead but Diligent**

Dearest Dead but Diligent,

Your employer should be willing to accommodate your
changing needs. Depending on where you live, your
employer should be able to at least enter a discussion
with you about accommodations. It doesn't hurt to ask,
especially if you come to the conversation with some
solutions. If you fear a difficult conversation, seek out help
from either HR or a local disability organization.

    If your employer reacts poorly, simply turn the entire
company into vampires. Then, you can all enjoy the moonlight together.

> Sincerely,
> **Austere Advisor**

Dear Lurid Letter Writer,

Just like Wednesday, I'd like to be a writer. I want to write about terrifying things, but my school will only read to us from the collections of Dr. Seuss. What can I do to learn about the craft of gothic writing?

Much love,
Aspiring Author

My great Aspiring Author,

How cruel of your learning establishment. As Morticia despairingly notes of *The Cat in the Hat* while reading it to her son Pubert in the 1993 film *Addams Family Values*, "Oh no. He lives."

To be fair to your underpaid and overworked instructors, many teachers are limited in what they are allowed to teach you in your classroom. However, there is a beautiful underworld of literature lurking in your local library. Additionally, many of the early classics are available online—completely legally. We will give you detailed instructions on ancient literature heists in a private scroll delivered to your nearest willow tree.

The Addamses love literature. They have a grand library filled with dusty tomes. In the 1991 film, their books have a bit of a magical bent. For example, when *Gone with the Wind* is opened, a wild gust of wind blasts from its pages. Fester bonds with the children while reading a family-friendly book called *Wounds, Scars, and Gouges*. We hope the pictures were informative.

Let's explore some of the foundational classics of literature. Aside from the many Shakespearean death scenes, Wednesday and the Addamses look to the gothic classics. Most notably referenced in the *Wednesday* television show, Edgar Allan Poe is an important figure within both the literary canon and the Addams family. He was an alumnus of Wednesday's Nevermore Academy, and many of his works inspired his namesake challenge, the Poe Cup. Some of our personal favorites of his work include "The Raven," "The Fall of the House of Usher," and the "Tell-Tale Heart." His short story "The Cask of Amontillado" is both a central text of the gothic as well as a handy guide for how to deal with insults.

Please, peruse the classics of the genre, such as *Dracula* by Bram Stoker, *Frankenstein* by Mary Shelley, and *Rebecca* by Daphne du Maurier. Memorize the bibliographies of writers such as Shirley Jackson, Toni Morrison, and Carmen Maria Machado. After you have learned from the masters, apply the gothic to your own insidious inventions.

Write whatever blackens your heart, and a hoard of devoted readers are sure to follow.

With a curse of ambition,

Lurid Letter Writer

P.S. It has come to our attention via our lawyers that the recommended reading may be a higher level than the letter writer currently reads at, seeing as his school reads primarily picture books. We disagree, but as a compromise, here is a recommended spooky reading list for younger readers:

† *Goosebumps* by R. L. Stein
† *Small Spaces* by Katherine Arden
† *Hide & Seeker* by Daka Harmon
† *The Nest* by Kenneth Oppel

Reader, beware...

My Horrible Helper,

I have recently begun my new career as a house flipper. I am so excited to take modern houses and turn them into uniquely terrifying homes! However, I've been receiving a lot of negative feedback about my hard work. Things like, "You're ruining the value of the neighborhood" and "Why are you introducing so many spiders in the backyard?" and "Who needs that much black paint?" I'm beginning to feel very discouraged. What do you think?

From,

Freaky Flipper

My misunderstood Freaky Flipper,

Your aesthetic instincts sound beautiful and well-tailored for the worst of us. My concern is that perhaps you are in the wrong community or area of town. Upsetting the delicate ecosystem of an established neighborhood will often lead to unhappy locals. Although we'd personally welcome more spiderwebs in the community, perhaps consider the ramifications. Would the spiders like living in such a clean-cut area?

This may be a situation in which you need to know your audience. Wednesday would be delighted by the improvements you've made to your homes, but she'd have little interest in living in the middle of a suburb. Have you checked for abandoned lighthouses on cliffs, or perhaps a singular tower on the wailing moors?

Lonesomely yours,
Horrible Helper

Hello Haunter,

I'm on a sports team in college, and the coach suggests we all have an online presence. It's not required, but I'm kind of interested—even if I'm not really the influencer type. My teammates are all pretty great and encourage me to sink my teeth in, but they're so perky and positive, and their social media pages are all about affirmations and cute outfits. I don't think I can do that, but I want to join them. Help!

Love,
Not Perky Player

Dear Not Perky,

We recommend typing your thoughts on a haunted typewriter and posting them around campus with miniature oil portraits of yourself. Include no means of contacting you and accept no commentary on your posts. That should satisfy both your coach and your desire to join your teammates.

Sincerely,
Haunter

Dear Not Perky,

Our intern explained to us what "social media" means.
While we find this sort of vulnerability to be unbecoming,
we are intrigued by the idea of influencing a mass amount
of people to appreciate your chosen cult, even if it is such
a thing as organized sport. Allow us to look through some
notable influencers and reassess the situation...

...Well. We had expected the grim devotion to capitalism, but the curated pastels to indicate joy and prosperity
have shaken us to our core. We will need a moment to
gather ourselves before we are able to continue. We will
have to dictate the rest of this letter to our intern from our
fainting couch.

Clearly, the influencing space needs your unique
voice. The affirmations alone are quite limited. When you
prepare for an upcoming sporting event, should you tell
yourself, "I can do it, I am enough"? Hardly! Tell yourself,
"The blood of my enemies will not satiate my bloodlust
for long. There is a darkness within me that will never be
satisfied. This win will bring only fleeting comfort, but it
will be comfort nonetheless." Use your *own* affirmations.
If they help you, they will help other young athletes with
unusual tastes. While you love your teammates, think of
how you feel different from them. The ability to reach out
to others like you will be valuable.

If fashion is of interest to you, post your fashion choices, though they may consist of mourning gowns and matching veils. This may not match the attire of the rest of the ghouls on your team, but that means your unique sartorial choices will drive curiosity and clicks.

If you want to share your story, do so. Every voice in the haunting Gregorian chant leads to a more ominous song. Your voice may be unique, which often makes it all the more meaningful.

We still do not approve of the concept of "likes." Horrible. How dare they.

Sincerely,
Haunter

Dear Creepy Comrade,

I am a well-respected ophthalmologist, and I provide a unique red-eye treatment in which my patients receive permanent red eyes. They are very pleased with their new look. However, my coworkers at my practice are very jealous. They no longer invite me to social gatherings, and when I walk into the break room, they stop talking. I am proud of my work, but I miss having a good relationship with my colleagues.

Thank you,
Eye See You

Dear Eye See You,

Thank you for your ominous sign-off. We appreciated the chills down our spine.

We are sorry to hear about your rude colleagues. It is deeply unfortunate that adults continue to harbor the same feelings of inadequacy and insecurity that plagued us as teenagers. Wednesday, herself, battles the ugly emotions of her peers. For instance, the talented siren Bianca Barclay, used to being the best at everything at Nevermore Academy, instantly dislikes our hardened heroine. She attempts to sabotage Wednesday at every turn, from botany class to the Poe Cup. She ultimately overcomes her jealousy by admitting she feels jealous of Wednesday's ability to ignore what people think of her. Bianca, as a siren, feels like she cannot be her true self while people constantly doubt her intentions. After this confession, Bianca and Wednesday become allies in their fight to protect Nevermore.

Unfortunately, people in the real world are rarely as self-reflective and honest as the wonderful Bianca. We cannot expect your colleagues to admit to themselves their true feelings, as most people are cowards. So we must examine your own options. You can react in a few different manners.

Take a cue from Wednesday and millions of other employed people and ignore your coworkers. They are merely other cogs in the crushing machine of capitalism and have little impact on the parts of your life that matter: spending time with loved ones, resting with your favorite hobbies, and raising demonic forces. Try to place their rudeness aside and act as if you do not notice. One of the best defenses the Addamses have is their complete obliviousness to others' disdain. There are countless examples of the Addamses being their true selves and having no awareness of their dull neighbors' opinions. The Addamses are some of the happiest characters ever created because of their total devotion to being themselves. Your coworkers' inability to be gracious is their burden. Act as if you don't notice their rudeness for long enough, and you will find yourself genuinely caring no longer. Place your energies in your clients and your loved ones. And the demons, naturally.

We are unsure of the structure of your office, and we do not care to check, but if you have a boss or HR, consider bringing this concern to them. If you have evidence of workplace toxicity, they may be able to help mediate a conversation to bring the office back to civility. (As a side note, "mediate" does not mean contacting the dead in a professional setting. We've been disappointed to know, so we wanted to give you a forewarning.)

There is one...kind option. If you have an influx of clients wanting this red eye treatment and you are unable to see all of them yourself, you could invite one of your coworkers to assist you. Ugh, we hate this one. Utilize peace only as a last option.

Our last and favorite suggestion is to place a curse upon all of them. We have many favorite curse recommendations, including a classic mass hysteria of a dancing plague. We will send these to you by hiding riddles in the texts of your favorite books.

Happy reading,
Creepy Comrade

Dear Darkest Day of the Week,

My friend has recently begun working in a sales business in which she sells some colorful leggings. In order to move up in the business, she needs to recruit people under her who then sell and recruit more sellers under *them*. She really wants me to join, but I don't think I'm very good at talking to people. She says we'll both become millionaires. Do you think I should take the plunge?

Love,
Black Leggings Only

Dear Black Leggings Only,

We have little interest in pyramids without mummies and cursed amulets inside, but this sounds like a very similarly shaped scheme. You're too low on the pyramid scheme to take advantage of thousands of people; you'd likely only be able to manipulate dozens. Not worth the work.

Burn the leggings. Convince your friend to instead rob famous museums and return the artifacts to their country of origin. And some jewels for yourself, of course.

Love,
Darkest Day

NOTE: Our lawyers once again want us to say we are joking. We love jokes.

CHAPTER 4
MANNERS & KEEPING THE HOME

Introduction

Have you ever heard of Emily Post? Emily Post was a writer who became famous for her tomes on etiquette and manners. She wrote a best-selling book on etiquette in 1922, as well as a column on "good taste." She offered instructions on how to appropriately behave in public, such as when a gentleman should remove his hat versus just lift it, phrases to avoid in good society, and even how to behave properly at the opera (she claims it is inappropriate to giggle there, obviously), We sadly do not know what Emily Post would think of Wednesday Addams, but we do think Wednesday and all of the Addams would have strong opinions on the idea of etiquette and manners.

When a young gothic socialite has questions on the best way to set a table for the summer solstice, to whom should she turn? When a handsome monster wants to know the best way to clean his coffin, whom could he possibly ask? Don't our dark companions also have questions to answer in regard to society? Perhaps someone wants to greet their new neighbor who wails into the night—what is the best way to do so?

While it may seem counterintuitive to seek the Addamses' advice in this regard, as we frequently see them threatening strangers for their own amusement, the Addamses also demonstrate welcoming attitudes toward their neighbors. In the following section, we will look to their example as we work on answering questions about the spookiest of etiquette rules as well as keeping a wonderfully unhappy home.

Dear Woeful Witch,

I just started dating someone new. I'm a vampire and while eating, I spilled some blood on their white carpet. How can I fix this?

Your friend,
Vampire Valentine

Dear Vampire Valentine,
Add more blood.

From,
Woeful Witch

To the Grumpy Girl,

I recently purchased my first home! I'm so excited to finally get to decorate in the way I've always wanted. My dream home is to have that Wednesday flair. How can I achieve that gothic look?

Thank you!
Hopeful Homeowner

Hello Homeowner,

Congratulations on your new home. We can only hope that it is a death trap that you can truly make your own. Let's take a look at some of the iconic Addams family décor touches, from the miserable mansion to the dark dorm of Nevermore.

The family home is a dilapidated mansion located on 0001 Cemetery Lane. The exterior is most often based on the original cartoon by Charles Addams—a big, dark manor with a tall tower and roof from which the family will occasionally pour boiling oil onto carolers. The television show displays an eclectic interior of oddities, from a stuffed moose head (with a back end serving as a clock in another room) to a mounted fish with a human leg sticking from its mouth. Consider adding a statement chair, such as

Morticia's iconic wicker throne with a flared back, known as a peacock chair.

Ornate furnishings are a must. On the whole, most versions of the house contain dark woods with decorative elements, jewel tones to offset the necessary black, and unique lighting fixtures. If you are going to have a library, make sure the floor-to-ceiling bookshelves are stacked with vintage grimoires, and of course one of them should lead to a hidden opening (leading to your vault of doubloons is only one idea). Cobwebs dripping from every corner are not only an aesthetic marvel but are a safe haven for your many arachnids. Richly colored textiles like velvet make for a nice touch.

While the whole home is cohesive, be sure to allow for individuality. Wednesday's room tends to be Victorian inspired, while Pugsley's features multiple road signs he's stolen. Additionally, making sure your swords are displayed properly will be both beautiful and useful if you are attacked by an interloper.

In the Netflix show *Wednesday*, we see Wednesday's side of the dorm room as austere and colorless, just as we like. The most iconic piece of her dorm room is the circular spiderweb-like window, with a colorful side representing her roommate Enid. Wednesday's side of the room contains a dark leather armchair, a faded oriental rug, and her beautiful black cello in a spot of honor. Wednesday also includes some vintage touches: her trusty typewriter on her wooden writer's desk and a beautiful gramophone. The witchy side of her family is represented in a crystal ball on her desk, in a carrying case that resembles one of the turrets from the family mansion.

In all versions of the Addams family, their decor contains beautifully framed paintings. The original show features an oil portrait of a giraffe in a tuxedo (a family ancestor), and the halls of Nevermore are covered in unique portraits. Wednesday even has a framed portrait of her beloved tarantula. Finding some gothic and quirky prints to display will help bring your home to the deepest depths of the uncanny.

One of our favorite details of the Addams family home is the sign on the iron gate, stating BEWARE OF THE THING. We encourage you to display something similar. After all, a warning is only fair.

With style,
Grumpy Girl

Dear Mysterious Misery,

I have recently begun my career as a rideshare driver. I'd like to be welcoming to my passengers, but I prefer to communicate through grunts and moans. What can I do to make them feel comfortable in my hearse?

Thank you,
Shy Rideshare

Sweet Shy Rideshare,

You remind me of our dear butler, Lurch. Although the family often comments on his eloquence of speech, we as the viewers very rarely hear Lurch utter more than grunts. We do think his catchphrase of "You rang?" may be a good way to greet passengers upon arrival.

Lurch is the star of many an Addams family adventure, and is often depicted as one of Wednesday's best friends. She attempts to teach him to dance in a couple of episodes of the 1960s television show. Throughout the oeuvre of the Addams family, Lurch has wooed ladies, become a pop star, and mastered the harpsichord, all while remaining a devoted and intimidating honorary member of the family. He accomplishes so much yet remains fairly reserved.

So how does Lurch do it? Lurch is arguably the gentlest member of the family (perhaps along with Thing), with his unending loyalty and the amount of care he puts into his relationship with each member of the family. His ability to listen and show understanding of his family's needs make Lurch one of the most valuable people in their lives.

We can tell by your desire to make your customers comfortable that you have some of that innate gentleness. While ordinarily we'd tell you to ignore that and follow your more vicious instincts, we think your concern for strangers is admirable. Offer them some amenities—bottled water, gum, the souls of the innocent—and listen if they talk. Our favorite rides are always dead silent, which makes the back of your hearse perfect. However, they may be seeking a listener to share their burdens. Listen, nod, and learn the following phrases: "You're right," "You don't say?" and, most important of all, "That sucks." Learn when to use them, and wield them wisely.

May you drive with wild abandon,
Mysterious Misery

Dear Rotten Writer,

I have become obsessed. I stay up all night to study the stars to interpret the prophecy. I am single-minded in my pursuit. I am a madwoman. But to my consternation, I do not *look* like a madwoman. I do not have bags under my eyes, and my hair is not wild. My friends and coworkers treat me as if I were completely normal. I am so frustrated. How can I make my outsides as wild as my insides?

Thank you,
Obsessed but Beautiful

Dear Obsessed but Beautiful,

We understand your frustration. Prophecies are so important, but we would like our hard work to be recognizable to others. Unluckily for people around the world who must learn to manage unachievable beauty standards, makeup is a wonderful tool. We see Morticia with glamorous makeup. In fact, in the 2019 animated film, we see Morticia using her mother's ashes as her glitzy eyeshadow. So sustainable! In the Netflix television series, Wednesday has a softer, grungier style of makeup than her mother but still achieves a gothic look.

All this to say, you can make yourself look however you'd like. If you don't have access to makeup, we're sure you're aware of the ways to make pigmented powder from the petals of your various carnivorous flowers. Makeup is used to enhance your natural beauty, so simply darken the natural rings under your eyes with a light dusting of dark eyeshadow. If you wish to accentuate the pallor of your obsessive visage, use a foundation a shade or two lighter than your natural color. Be sure to blend into your neck; a mismatch of shades is sure to bring your ruse into light.

Aside from makeup, be sure to include some subtle new habits into your everyday mannerisms. Look out the window and mutter, "When the moon rises..." and fade into ominous silence. Any time anyone does anything of note, be sure to mention, "As the prophecy foretold." (Even if the prophecy has not specifically mentioned your coworker Claire stubbing her toe, we assume that Claire's injury could fall under the general woe of the world.) If you are required to wear a certain uniform during your every-day life (and are not, for example, permitted to wear your Victorian nightgown with dripping candelabra), try adding a hint or two of your more mystical traits. An amulet, for instance, is often a statement piece and a conversation starter. Of course, try to restrict your comments to prophe-cy-related remarks, such as, "The curse requires a vessel."

Dear Miserable Madam,

I have been invited to a wedding that I unfortunately cannot attend. The groom is the son of a beloved friend. My friend will be sad I cannot make it, but I do not think her son will be particularly upset. It was very sweet of them to invite me, and I would like to let them know that I'm grateful for the invitation, even if I can't make it.

Additionally, what do young newlywed couples need nowadays? They have a registry, but maybe I should be more creative with my gift.

Thank you,
RSVP No

Dear RSVP No,

We appreciate how thoughtful you are with this issue. It's clear that you have a fondness for your friend and her family. Be wary about sharing your weakness for them publicly—it will let your enemies know where your soft spots are. Even we are taking notes, just in case you wrong us later.

To answer your question, give your friend and her son each a call. Let them know what you told us, that you are grateful but are unable to make it. The groom will certainly understand and move on to some sidelined friends to invite in your place. You seem to be sure that your friend will be upset. In this case, tell her first lest her son break the news in a careless manner. Take her to lunch if you think this will help ease any hurt feelings. Assure her of your affection for her and her son. She is of course allowed to be disappointed, but any histrionics or rudeness toward you should not be tolerated. If she overreacts with angry tirades or guilt trips, repeat your disappointment that you must miss the wedding and then end the conversation. We find a handkerchief dipped in chloroform is a successful tool in this case.

Do not be creative with your gift. Order from the registry. If you'd like to be creative, learn to paint or take a pottery class. Feel free to gift your creation in *addition* to a gift from the registry. Newlyweds know what they need better than you do.

However, your question gives us an opportunity to recommend things for newlyweds without a registry. For future reference, here are some acceptable gifts for newlyweds:

  † Tools and seeds for the new garden. Don't forget belladonna, it's a crucial poison for any beginning garden.

† Matching urns. It will give them something to look forward to. Be sure the urns are in their preferred style, so that they will not look unusual on the mantle.

† An oil portrait. Providing a bound and gagged artist will help save them so much time on choosing and stalking an artist. Perhaps the portraitist will be able to paint a scene of the wedding as it's happening—"live paintings" at weddings are so trendy these days!

† A colony of spiders. Think of how clean and bare their new cupboards and corners are. Black widows would be particularly thoughtful, as every new bride admires a widow.

† If they do not have a generational or family curse, providing them with a cursed amulet would be very thoughtful. Not everyone is close with their family, and providing such an item could be a lovely way to start their own family memories.

Best of luck with your friend, and her son's impending nuptials. Love (and weddings) can be so dreadful.

Matrimonially,

Miserable Madam

Awful Advisor,

I would like a full style overhaul and dress like an Addams. Advise me in the building of a truly frightening fashion.

Hairstyles would also help.

From,
New Look

Dear New Look,

Outward appearances are nothing. Our bodies are but cursed vessels for our souls. We are merely ghosts, haunting our bodies until we are able to haunt a home in the afterlife. Do not concern yourself with the best way to adorn your flesh prison, focus instead on making sure your inner self is as tortured and miserable as possible. If you do wish to adorn your dark visage, we understand. Read on for some of our favorite Addams aesthetic tips.

Let's tackle wardrobe first. We do not think you need to bankrupt yourself for these clothing items. The Addamses live quite sustainably, and many of them have been wearing the same outfits since 1938. Thrift or consignment stores are great places to find staple wardrobe pieces, as well as cursed dolls. We also love the idea of handmaking these items—Morticia has been seen creating pieces for her children, and Wednesday's roommate, Enid, makes a snood for her.

Wardrobe is primarily black. As Morticia says, it's just such a happy color. Most Addamses wear all black, with some white accents. To achieve a Morticia look, glamorous goth is the way to go. Morticia wears long black dresses with a tight-fitted "hobble" skirt (named thusly for the hobbling gait it caused the wearer) and long fabric tentacles crawling along the floor. In some versions of Morticia, she wears little to no jewelry; in others, she wears a crystal pendant or jeweled ring. Morticia's hair is, like the rest of her family's, jet black. She wears it very long and straight, with a sharp middle part. Morticia's makeup is one of the most iconic parts of her ensemble: red lips and nails, with a perfect smoky eye.

If your tastes lean toward so-called menswear (which we argue can be worn by any gender), let's discuss Gomez and Pugsley. Gomez wears dark pinstripe suits. He often holds a cigar, though we recommend finding a less lethal accessory. If this sounds like an expensive ensemble, you'd be correct. According to *Forbes*, Gomez spends $1,000 a month on cigars. If this seems like too much work for an outfit, let's turn our attention to the most casually costumed member of the family: Pugsley. Pugsley usually wears long shorts paired with a black and white striped

T-shirt. The animated films allow Pugsley *some* color, with red and white stripes. He often carries around explosives, which also seems slightly too lethal for a casual accessory. We leave this to your discretion. For short-haired people looking to emulate the family, Gomez usually has slicked hair with a middle part (occasionally swept back instead), and an iconic pencil mustache. Pugsley's hair often appears to be a traditional boy's cut or buzzed, though his Netflix portrayal has a wonderful 'do with a side part curling onto his forehead.

Now let's look to Wednesday's multiple styles within her familiar aesthetic. Most commonly, Wednesday wears a black dress with a white pointed collar. She tends to like button-up dresses, and occasionally the long-sleeved versions of this dress have wrist cuff collars as well. All of Wednesday's collars are sharp and crisp. She wears black nail polish and usually a neutral lip color, with an occasional black or dark lip. We get to see more variations of Wednesday's ensemble in the Netflix adaptation. Wednesday wears strictly black and white (as she is "allergic to color"). She wears black and white stripes and checkerboard patterns in the forms of sweaters or oversized vests, as well as black pants or shorts. She even wears black-and-white striped socks to go with her chunky platform shoes—also black, of course. Wednesday does wear a delightfully dark ball gown, with black ruffles and a black collar. In many other variations of the character, Wednesday does experiment with color. She tries wearing a pink barrette in the animated film, and a yellow dress in the Broadway adaptation.

Wednesday's hair is perhaps the most iconic piece of her ensemble. She wears her hair in two long braids, with a middle part or topped with bangs. In a move that does cause us physical pain, the musical features a scene in which she cuts her braids. We don't like to talk about it. We will, however, talk you through how to do Wednesday's classic braids.

Part your hair down the middle, with an equal amount of hair on both sides. Divide one half of your hair into three equal sections. Keeping these separate with your fingers will be the most difficult part of the process, but we have faith in your ability. Cross the right section of hair over the center strand, so it is now in the middle. Then take the left strand and move that over to the middle—now this is the middle strand. Continue this pattern, moving the right and left strands of hair into the center, weaving them over each other. Tie off when you are pleased with the length of the braid. Repeat for your other section of hair. If you'd like a thicker look to your braids, you can *gently* tug at the sides of the braid to fan out the hair.

During the scene in the Netflix adaptation where Wednesday wears her gown, she has her hair in milkmaid braids. This is an easy but powerful hairstyle. Braid your hair into your traditional two braids with a middle part. Then place each braid up on top of your head and pin it behind the opposite ear. Do the same with the other braid, securing it behind the other ear. Experiment with the placement and the thickness of the braids. Use plenty of pins and a plethora of hairspray. This will keep it in place as you run from monsters.

Remember, outer beauty does not exist. The true horrors are on the inside.

Love,

Awful Advisor

To the Abhorrent Advisor,

Just as a hypothetical question—where does one bury
a body? And if that happens to hypothetically fail, how
would one escape prison?

No reason. Just wondering. Just a cool, little theoretical problem to speculate on.

Thanks!
Strong Alibi

To Strong Alibi,

Please learn subtlety. We don't think we can help you,
as you would immediately hypothetically reveal us as an
accomplice. Hiding a body is one of the first things we
would expect you to know, and we feel that if we give you
the answer you will never learn for yourself. It's not your
fault if your family never taught you the basics, but do
some independent research. The library is free, and surely
so are many local crypts.

As for your second question, if you have to ask how to
escape prison, you'll never know.

The Addamses, as you may imagine, have a history of
committing murder and going to prison. We see this most
explored in the Netflix adaptation, where we discover that

Morticia may have murdered a classmate in self-defense when she was a student at Nevermore. Gomez, Morticia, and Wednesday all spend some time in the Jericho jail. Wednesday is clever enough to have evidence in her jacket to exonerate them, but we doubt you'll have the foresight to carry such useful items on your person.

One of Gomez's many careers, as you may remember, is that of a defense attorney. We could give you his number, as he has a perfect case record. Meaning, of course, that while he has never lost a case, he has never won one either. His nickname is Gomez "Loophole" Addams for a reason, after all.

We wish you hypothetical luck. We do not relate to you because we have never been accused of such a crime. We've never been caught.

Remorsefully yours,

Abhorrent Advisor

NOTE: Our lawyers have so many things to say about this letter that they've asked us to just strike it from the record. We're not sure how to do that, so just pretend you've forgotten everything we've said here. Our letter should wash away in a black tide immediately after you've read it, so there will be little evidence. As always, we are very thorough.

My Fearsome Friend,

My children are about to come of age and are ready to be presented to our scary society. In our circles, we highly value dance. What should I do to prepare my children in this awful art form?

Thank you,
Papa Promenade

Papa Promenade,

Oh, dancing. Gomez asked Morticia once, "How long has it been since we waltzed?" And Morticia responds despondently, "Oh Gomez. Hours."

We recommend you never force someone to dance, unless it is an exquisite form of torture involving red-hot iron shoes as in some of the more gruesome fairy tales. Assuming your children are inclined toward the craft of the conga, please read on. (Also, we are joking about the conga. It is not very elegant, is it?)

The Addamses love to dance. Perhaps this surprises you, as people may assume they would prefer more somber activities such as fencing or croquet with grenades. This may be true, but the Addamses have a special fondness for dance. Gomez and Morticia famously dance frequently in their relationship, often performing their own variation of the tango. Their passion for each other translates well into dance, with an excess of arm kisses, twirling, and knife throwing.

The Addamses know some traditional dances as well. In the 1990s version of the family, Gomez encourages Fester to join him in a performance of the Mamushka. It's a feat of brotherly love that involves singing, dancing, and sword-swallowing. In the 2019 animated film, Pugsley is gearing up for his initiation ceremony of the Mazurka. The Mazurka involves sword-fighting and a finger-snapping dance. We are very fond of the fact that many of the traditional familial dances contain swords. The 1992 animated series also mentions several family dances, including the Rattlesnake Toxin Tumble and the Bat Bite Jubilee.

Wednesday, herself, as you may know, is a very competent dancer. In the original sitcom, Wednesday teaches Lurch to dance in at least two instances. She attempts to teach him ballet (in a black tutu, of course) in the episode "Lurch Learns to Dance," and later some more modern moves in "Lurch's Grand Romance." The latter is the most recognizable for the original Wednesday's dancing, having become popular on the internet as a meme. Of course, this has now been overshadowed by a new Wednesday dance routine that exploded onto the internet in 2022. If you look closely at Wednesday's stand-out dance in the Netflix adaptation, you will see some hidden references to this original dance. Choreographed by Jenna Ortega herself, the now-iconic dance takes reference from rock band Siouxsie and the Banshees, goth dancers in the '80s, and the original Wednesday dance from "Lurch's Grand Romance." Her carefully constructed dance has led to a social media craze, a viral ice-skating routine, and countless choreography tutorials on the internet.

Dancing can be a healthy form of self-expression. Find which form of dance speaks to your children. Does your child show an interest in glamor and elegance? Go for one of the traditional ballroom dances. Be sure to find a suitable black outfit, however. Is your child interested in your family culture? Do some research and try to find a cultural dance studio near you. Hopefully, your child shows a passion for sabers and blood, and you can teach one of the Addams dances. If your child has a penchant for morbidity and gothic subcultures, go ahead and teach them Jenna Ortaga's Wednesday dance. We do hope you enjoy listening to the Cramps.

Goo goo muck,
Your Fearsome Friend

Dear Weekday Witch,

I am so excited to be hosting my first dinner party. I'd love to know what to serve. I'm a pretty good cook, but I've never made anything for an occasion like this. What should I serve at my event?

Thank you!
Hungry Host

Hello Hungry Host,

Congratulations on this accomplishment of having friends over. We're sure you've achieved all the dreams your parents ever had for you.

Lucky for you, Wednesday and her family are connoisseurs of fine cuisine. Morticia makes sure her children are well behaved at the table, encouraging Wednesday to "play with [her] food." Below are some suggestions from the various television show, movies, and some personal favorites.

For appetizers, consider: fingers (fish, chicken, or if your friends do not eat animals, human), entrails, eye of tadpole, glutton bread, salamander puffs, gorgon-zola salad, deviled eggs.

For meals, consider: Morticia's baked eye of newt from when she attempted to join the Ladies' League, fricassee of toad, breast of alligator with henbane sauce, Mama's spécialité de la maison (be sure to start with the eyes), casserole of spleen (best served with a pinch of hemlock, scorpion pâté with belladonna sauce, bat broth, sweet and sour scorpion stew.

For desserts, consider: Wednesday's chocolate birthday cake, toadstool souffle, cookies (made from real Girl Scouts), porcupine taffy, poison caramel apple.

As for drinks, the Addamses have an impressive wine cellar. They also indulge in other drinks, such as hemlock cocktails.

For more ideas, Charles Addams released an Addams family cookbook entitled *Chas Addams Half-Baked Cookbook*. For Wednesday-specific recipes, please refer to our other book, *The Unofficial Wednesday Cookbook*. There are no poisons involved. We trust that you know when to add that extra-special kick and when to refrain from leaving evidence.

Bon appétit,
Weekday Witch

To the Creepy Counselor,

I'm about to begin my first job as a babysitter! I'm so excited. I'll be watching kids of all ages. Do you have any recommendations for games to play?

Love,
Beginning Babysitter

Dear Beginning Babysitter,

As Gomez says, "I hope one day you will know the indescribable joy of having children, and of paying someone else to raise them."

Our lawyers did not want us to respond to this letter. They thought we would give you inappropriate ideas that will lead to lawsuits and bodily harm to children. We asked if we could give you some information on what games the Addamses like to play, and they agreed so long as we warn you that no child should ever be exposed to the deranged dangers of an Addams family pastime. We will try to give you more "appropriate" and "safe" ideas at the end of our letter.

Pugsley and Wednesday have the most lovely games amongst themselves! Sometimes Wednesday will shoot an apple in Pugsley's mouth with an arrow, or see if he can survive in an electrocution chair in a romp charmingly titled "Is There a God?" The whole family enjoys a rousing seance or a game of wake the dead in their graveyard. They enjoy simple games with the baby of the family, such as seeing if he can bounce if they drop him from the roof to reenact executions of the French revolution. The family also enjoys playing darts and throwing knives (mostly at each other).

Here are some game ideas that involve little to no risk of serious injury, if you're interested in such things:

† Dolls. In most adaptations, Wednesday's beloved, beheaded doll Marie Antoinette is her most faithful companion. You can even eliminate the guillotine if you're so cautious.

† Arts & crafts. Making a portrait and then cutting the eyes out so you can spy on people as they walk by should be a fun little craft for your young friends.

† Listening to music and dancing. As described elsewhere in this book, the Addamses love to dance. We don't know what dancing is like without knives and swords. Hardly seems amusing.

Dear Friendly Foe,

A friend of mine is very mad at me. I love parties, so I offered to throw his birthday party, and he said yes! He doesn't like cheer or big crowds, but I did my best to make a party that people would like. I held his party at his house, even though the house is super dark and weird. He always decorates it with dark paintings and black curtains and stuff. I decorated it with colorful streamers and I displayed a cupcake tower with lots of cupcakes. I know he doesn't like cupcakes very much, but it's supposed to be a party and I wanted most people to be happy.

I had everyone gather outside in the backyard, and we danced to my favorite playlist, which has a lot of good music! He didn't even try to have fun; he just stood and sulked in corners and doorways. I worked really hard on the party and he just got mad at me for it.

What did I do wrong?

Party Monster

To Party Monster,

Well, we are a bit speechless. You offered to do this for your friend. It was supposed to be a kindness. We want to remind you that you were throwing a party for *your friend*, not for you. While you may enjoy colorful and tacky streamers, you know your friend prefers darker decor. While you may like cupcakes, your friend does not. You say you wanted to please a large number of the partygoers, but it is a party in honor of your friend.

Look back on the people you invited to your friend's birthday. Do they love and want to celebrate your friend? Assuming that you invited mutual friends that know and love your friend as he is, they would theoretically know what to expect from a party surrounding your friend. If your friend's favorite food is pizza with spider eggs, you could have ordered one pizza for him and some other boring pizzas for the other partygoers.

You say your friend's home is dark with heavy curtains and he does not like cheer and crowds. Is it possible that your friend does not enjoy spending time *outside* and *dancing* with a large number of people? Once again, it is a party for your friend. You can dance to your playlist on your birthday. We suspect your friend would have preferred to have a quiet, low-key seance, indoors.

When Wednesday's friends throw her a surprise birthday party in her Netflix series, they do not bring her to a noisy club. (Though she does not want a party in general, so one may argue they ignored all her wishes.) Her family knows her well, and when she was a child they threw her a party that she would be sure to love: all black decor, a deliciously macabre cake with a guillotine on top, and a spider pinata. We are afraid to even ask how many spiders were at your friend's party. You likely forgot to include them.

Apologize to your friend. Be honest. Tell him you were thinking of yourself instead of him. In penance, offer to theme your birthday party around what he would like. We do like how confusing this would be. You may disagree with our assessment. If you find yourself unable to admit your selfish nature, you may as well revel in it and go a step further. Begin ignoring all of your friends' feelings. Why even bother with friends, when you would be just as happy celebrating yourself every day? You will find yourself with no attendees at your birthday, however. We hope they will instead be giving your friend the party he actually wants.

With all the spiders in the pinata,

Friendly Foe

Conclusion

Dearest Addams Fan,

I've read all your letters and taken all of your advice to heart. My problem is, I still don't feel like an Addams! I've done everything I can, but I still just feel like me. What can I do?

Thanks,

Wannabe Wednesday

My Woeful Wannabe,

We weep for your hurt feelings. We realize we have clearly expressed the most important part of our advice: be yourself. Does this sound trite? Perhaps, but this advice is evergreen for a reason. We give you all these tools not to morph yourself into a Wednesday clone, but to take as guidance. We urge you to take these ideas and filter them through your own unique lens. It is possible to take inspiration from Wednesday and make it your own.

Perhaps you love Wednesday's signature white collar, but you have difficulty wearing an all-black outfit. Keep the collar and add it to your own monochromatic outfit with your personal favorite color. Or keep the black outfit, and add a pop of color in the collar.

Or perhaps you want to incorporate some of Wednesday's macabre personality, but your day-to-day life prevents you from indulging in your darker impulse. Maybe your job requires you to look and act in a way deemed "professional," or perhaps you live with family members who don't understand your dark desires. Or maybe you find yourself flirting with the gothic, but are not interested in a complete commitment to the lifestyle. Find ways to entertain your wicked whims. Listen to some mysterious music or read a classic horror novel. Just a dash of the dark will help create a satisfying contrast in your life.

Maybe you like the Addams family but find that no matter how hard you try, spiders and bats only make you shiver in disgust. Really consider what it is about Wednesday and the Addams family that appeal to us all. It's their total devotion to being themselves. Each member of the family feels joy in expressing themselves and hardly notices the disbelieving stares and snide comments of their neighbors. Take some time to get to know yourself. Journal about what you find yourself drawn to, read about subjects that truly interest you, and indulge in how wonderful you are.

Consider who you are and enjoy it. If you can manage to include some dark magic with it, all the better for the rest of us.

With all of the deep and unknown horrors beyond our comprehension,

Iphigenia Jones

Acknowledgments

T hank you to the many Addams experts who helped me with details and exact plotlines from a myriad of properties—particularly the book *The Addams Family: An Evilution* by H. Kevin Miserocchi and the Addams Family fandom wiki, which always knew the name of a minor character I was trying to remember.

Thank you to my family, who have always supported and encouraged my kookiness. I learned from the best.

Thank you to Laura Anderson for letting me borrow her cat, Mosey, to write this book. Thank you to the Large family—Chrissy, you've been my favorite magical girl for decades.

Thank you to the Ulysses Press team, especially Casie Vogel, who has even the blackest part of my heart.